BREAKING WIND

FARTYN MORRESTER has always been a high flier. After an early series of experiments that involved a lighted taper and the total destruction of his school cycle sheds, he flew very high indeed. Expelled under a cloud and in bad odour with his long suffering parents, he was forced to go off around the world – working his passage all the way.

He now devotes himself to blow football and ballooning, and lives alone in the Essex marshes.

KIM DURDANT-HOLLAMBY learned at an early age the joys of being double barrelled. A graduate of the Royal College of Music, he gave his first public performance with the wind section of the Krakatoa Philharmonic at three. At five, he studied under Professor Kamikaze at the Sorebumme, but turned his back on success shortly after five-thirty. (Opening time.)

Having learned to turn the other cheek, he went on to become a big noise in the rock industry.

We want the contents of this book to reach you in perfect condition. Should you not be satisfied, please return, stating where and when inhaled, and we shall gladly send you a replacement. This guarantee does not affect your statutory rights under the Clean Air Act of 1956.

Breaking Wind

Martyn Forrester
& Kim Durdant-Hollamby

ARROW BOOKS

Arrow Books Limited
17–21 Conway Street, London W1P 6JD
An imprint of the Hutchinson Publishing Group

London Melbourne Sydney Auckland
Johannesburg and agencies throughout
the world

First published in 1984

©Martyn Forrester
and Kim Durdant-Hollamby 1984

Illustrations©The Hutchinson Publishing
Group 1984

Set in A.M. Compset Bembo by
Photobooks (Bristol) Ltd.

Printed and bound in Great Britain
by Anchor Brendon Limited, Tiptree, Essex

ISBN 0 09 935880 8

To the dogfondler within us all

Contents*

*Please note that this book is sold by volume not weight, and some settling of contents may have occurred during transit.

Introduction

As consultant intestinologists, we are often asked: 'Which of you rank dogs dealt that one?' or: 'Where am I? That was truly dreadful, and you should be struck off.'

True, we *are* probably two of the most highly qualified fizzicians in the land, yet there is no medical reason why the whole population shouldn't join in.

This book is here to help you. To show you how to burn better rubber. Drop better rats. To give you a hand in cutting the cake. Putting them down. Letting them off. Releasing. Gruffing. Traffing. Boffing. In short, going for it.

Read, digest, and outwardly project all the advice that is contained in this book, and you will find yourself boldly going for it where no man has gone for it before. You will become a dogfondler among dogfondlers.

With very little exertion on your part, a whole new world will open up for you. And your mother-in-law will never beg to be taken on a motoring holiday again. We must, however, clear the air on one issue here and now. We do not claim to have found the cure-all for social outcasts: Tina Brown's problems are entirely her own.

There's nothing we can do for the Chelsea wine bar set (or, as they are sometimes called, poofs). But they don't do much for us, either.

Could they unleash the potential to clear an entire carriage of the 8.15? No. But you could – perhaps within minutes of reading this introduction.

Before long, we might invite you to join BOFF, the British Order of Fart Fiends (motto: 'Bowels Open, Fart Freely'). In time, you could even enter the BOFF Hall of Flame, alongside such all-time greats as the milkmaid who burned down Chicago, and Joan of Fart, who burned herself out.

First however, you must solemnly swear that you will stick to the Boffer's Code: That it is better to give than to receive, that it is never too late to return to society a little of that which has been put your way.

So take a deep breath, and we shall begin.

This Book, and How To Use It

Even if you have enjoyed some basic, alimentary education, how can you reach dizzier heights, really make something of yourself? There is, after all, no such thing as a Bachelor of Farts degree – not even at the Open University. No employer operates a Day Release system: they well know that a Pork'n'Chutney or Salami on Brown never did much for labour relations.

And yet history is peppered with examples of extraordinary men (and women) breaking new frontiers – remember the Pilgrim Farters, William the Conkerer, the Magna Farta? Not to mention the singeing of the King of Spain's beard, the South Sea Bubble, or the Highland Clearances? Or, come to that, why Ethelred was so Unready and Ivan so Terrible, how Alfred burned the cakes and Harold got one in the eye, and exactly how Guy Fawkes proposed to blow up the Houses of Parliament?

You don't remember? Then we have much to do.

We must start at the bottom, from the first rumblings of creation, and work our way through to the explosive present. We will provide a blow-by-blow account of what you must do, where, when, how, with whom, and why. Just trust us completely and let yourself go.

A word of warning: farting is not as easy as it sounds. Some ignoranuses will tell you: farting is like singing, we can all carry a tune. Crap. There are many bar-room crooners in this world, but only one Pavarotti. So it is with farting. Yet if we can catch you young enough, who knows what glittering prizes might not be yours?

Yes, we'll make you sing all right. Just a minute or two from now, you could be belting your way through a solo with all the gusto, authority, flair and technical excellence that it takes to raise the roof and bring the house down.

But first things first. Have you the sheer, burning ambition to go for gold? Are you concerned about pollution? North Sea Gas? Inflation, deflation, The Snake, and whether to float the pound? Do you enjoy a really good economic boom?

Are you aware of The Yellow Peril and The Male Model? Do you applaud Ronald Raygun (he of 'Blazing Saddles' fame?) and his efforts on our behalf to have more fast breeder reactors, dump more waste and push more strongly for the zero option?

Do you despise Fartchi & Fartchi, yet admire their having groomed that most wondrous and powerful of all models, the Iron Lady? (Which comes over with such force and total absence of U-turns that after one of her all night sittings, the House finally rose at 2 a.m.)

Do you adhere to the belief that Michael Poot is full of hot air, and Labour Isn't Farting?

Would you like to be called Norman Fouler?

Or are you a weedy popper of a floating farter – dare we say it . . . a wet??

Are you full of twaddle about turning the cheek and the sacrifice of the Tolpuddle Farters? Do you hate South Africa just because of afartheid, and not because the damned place is foreign? Do you listen to farty political broadcasts when the socialists are on? Do you still harbour sympathy for that born-again popper, Jimmy Farter, and go on sit-ins for fart free zones and voluntary restraint?

Have you even heard of Wally Jumbo-Blat, let alone dislike him (again, on the grounds of being ineligible for membership of BOFF)?

It isn't all plain sailing, of course, being a dyed-in-the-wool farter of the old school. There are lots of people to look out for and to turn your nose up at: breakaways we call them, and they include juvenile pooh sniffers, Moonies (we believe it is better to pollute with a really decent boff than with the thoughts of fat Koreans), Smell's Angels, beach bums and The Silent Majority. (In fact the only minority groups you are allowed to like are Indians and Pakistanis, and that's because they're always open 24 hours – great for a bit of late night popping.)

As long as you're One Of Us, there is a point to your continued presence on this planet. As long, that is, as you're the kind of person that takes a hard line on leaks in the Cabinet (very much in favour). The sort of solid citizen that in 1984, the year of Fartspeak, welcomes with open arms the prospect of Doublestink, and looks forward very much to the inhalation of his very first Big Brother.

There's only one way to find out. Have a go at the penetrating quiz that follows. Be honest with yourself, so that we may discover together the rough edges that need smoothing, the talents that need bringing out, the bad habits that need to be suppressed.

Answer all the questions, under as near to exam conditions as possible – and remember that under no circumstances should you fart on both sides of the paper.

Now chocks away, chaps, and happy hunting!

Have You Got It In You?

1. How many times a day do you put one down?
(a) Less than 5.
(b) Over 300.
(c) Only once, but it's a real stoater.

2. How often do you go for it on a crowded train?
(a) Once a week.
(b) Twice a week.
(c) I don't commute, but have sent one in an envelope to Jimmy Savile.

3. Have you ever seen a volcano?
(a) I've never been to Italy.
(b) Yes, but it was extinct.
(c) Where am I?

4. Your partner complains about burning rubber. Do you:
(a) Change gear?
(b) Change underwear?
(c) Change partner?

5. Has anyone ever brought you a hot water bottle when you're taking a bath (see p. 56)?
(a) No.
(b) Yes.
(c) I am in solitary confinement.

6. You've taken your partner to see 'Love Story' for the sixth time. It is ten minutes from the end of the film and you gruff loudly. Do you:

(a) Say nothing, but blush.
(b) Say that you're sorry.
(c) Say that love means never having to say you're sorry.

7. Your partner fancies going for a burn. Do you:

(a) Get your car out?
(b) Get something else out?
(c) Lie on your back and get the Swan Vestas out?

8. You fill the office of managing director. Managing director very angry. Do you:

(a) Break down.
(b) Tell him that he who smelt it dealt it, and he's a rancid robot.
(c) Tell him that he who smelt it dealt it, he's a rancid robot, and could you have a rise?

9. If the balloon went up, would you:

(a) Bring up your bladder trouble?
(b) Bring up your breakfast?
(c) Bring up the rear?

10. Facing a heavy enemy bombardment, would you:

(a) Get shell shock?
(b) Say: 'We shall fart on the beaches . . .'?
(c) Wait till you could see the whites of their eyes, then let them have it from the hip?

11. An old flame suggests reliving some happy moments. Do you:

(a) Claim it's a breach of the fire regulations?
(b) Burn the candle at both ends?
(c) Burn yourself out?

12. Your partner finds out. Do you:
(a) Admit there's no smoke without fire?
(b) Bend over backwards to make amends?
(c) Add fuel to the flames?

13. You make it up, and decide to pop the question. Do you:
(a) Go down on bended knee and do the popping?
(b) Go down on bended knee, do the popping, and say: 'Will you marry me'?
(c) Go down on bended knee, drop an enormous Maiden's Prayer, and sing: 'Have you got a light, boy'?

14. When do you like to get up?
(a) At the crack of dawn?
(b) At sparrow's fart?
(c) At first light?

15. You are invited to a house warming and forget to ask about clothes. Do you:
(a) Play it by ear?
(b) Wear your fart on your sleeve?
(c) Set light to your sleeve and get on like a house on fire?

Score as follows:
(a) 1
(b) 10
(c) 1000

Well, how much did you manage?

Score 0–15
You're in serious trouble. Either study this book, or naff off back to the wine bar.

Score 15–150
You're up and coming – head a bit in the clouds, perhaps, but you should live to a ripe old age. Don't get too full of yourself though: it may just be a flash in the pan.

Score 150–15,000
Either you're a liar, or no, we *don't* want a lift to work.

FART ONE
The Fundamentals

'Give me somewhere to stand and I will move the earth.'

Arispopple

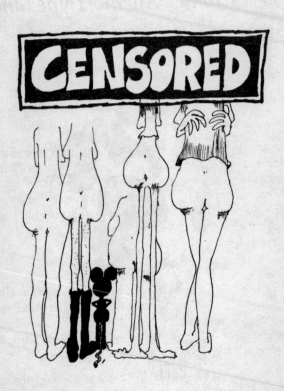

1
The Strong, Silent Type and Others

'The best laid rubber of mice and men
gang oft a-flame.'

Burns

We hope you don't feel deflated.

Rome was not built in a day. (And just ask Nero how
quickly a city can burn down when a ham-fisted
amateur uses too short a taper.)

So to get you off the ground, there now follows a
user's guide to the basic farts that will provide your
launch pad to future success.

1. The Bender (and family)

Truly one of the most vicious known to man, at first
acquaintance this model may appear quiet and un-
assuming, but don't be fooled. With one cunningly
placed Egg'n'Bacon Bender you'll have 52 empty seats
to choose from on your morning commute.

Sad to say, the Egg'n'Bacon Bender is an endangered
species (David Attenborough, please note), pushed out
by the rising cost of the great British breakfast – that,
and an upsurge in what are called convenience foods.
Better the devil you know, we say, even if it does mean
paying through the nose. Comprising any breakfast
foods eaten in combination, the Bender is an occupa-
tional hazard of commuting, in any country in the world.

Thus what may be an Egg'n'Bacon Bender on the 8.15 to Victoria, will be translated into a murderous Sweet'n'Sour Bender (or Kung Pooh) on the Orient Express, just as an Egg'n'Black Pudding Bender on the Flying Scotsman will be translated into a straightforward derailment.

It must be said that the Egg'n'Bacon Bender is a fairly middle-class phenomenon. More frequently encountered in the upper echelons of society is the dominant and stately Poached Haddock Wonder – unless, that is, the perpetrator saw active service in India. Then the offending item will in all probability be the Kedgeree Kaleidoscope (which will blow you straight back to the market place in Simla), or the dreaded Vindaloo Avenger (which is one step away from the Black Hole of Calcutta).

A feeble sub-species of the Bender which we would like you to turn your nose up at is the Warm'n'Toasty Waa-Waa. Most likely to cross your path on the District Line between Parsons Green and Mansion House, this model is instantly recognizable by the fact that it makes less noise than its owner. Not even with lime marmalade follow-through is this chinless little creep to be encouraged.

2. The Murmur

Hot on the heels of the Benders come their poor relations, the Murmurs. Put about by the Snap! Crackle! Pop! brigade of breakfast abusers, some of these apologetic early morning offerings don't even have the energy to crawl over a partition in an open plan office. Tragic stuff.

Among them are the shreddie'n'milk gargler (note, we don't even afford this one the dignity of capital letters), the Shredded Wheat Rustler (bet you can't do three), and that fave variant from Hampstead (why *is* their local paper called the Ham'n'High?), the Muesli'n'Honey Collective.

And don't forget to put your ear close to the telly next time there's a report from Greenham Common. You'll almost certainly be treated to one of those Whole Earthquakettes. We believe it's called the Whispering Rissole.

3. The Nasty Brute

Splash it on all over, but watch out for the lingering afterburn (and Henry Pooper). A close relative of the Turbo, but without the go-faster stripes.

4. The American Express

Want to go to Bahrain in a hurry? This will do nicely.

5. The Johnny Walker

Still going strong.

6. The Sloane Whinger

A storm in a teacup, this one, but so refained it's spelt with two small 'f's. Rumoured to be the reason why Peter Jones shuts early on a Saturday.

7. The Up-and-Under

With a bit of practice, you can let rip on your own twenty metre line and cut right into enemy territory. We've known some Welshmen who've started a movement with a dummy, and ended up dropping one right between the posts.

8. The Boomerang (alias the Bad Penny)

Throw a Boomerang and you've got a friend for life. They don't make much noise but by jingo do they honk. Just when you thought it was safe to go back in the water, the old Boomerang's back on its second lap.

This is the one you'll carry with you all night long, trapped in the seat of your Wranglers and out-staying its welcome like you won't believe.

If you're on a date and you send a Boomerang into orbit, your only hope is to feed your partner a late night pork'n'chutney sandwich, wait an hour or so, then rip off your clothes under cover of the fearsome bombardment.

Boomerangs *always* come back.

9. The Popper

Oh good grief. These give such a bad name to the art. Ask any limp-wristed drinker of Piesporter in a Chelsea wine bar and they'll tell you that a Popper is really 'a fartette'. This statement will be greeted by a chorus of giggling approval from all the other namby-pamby woofters in the vicinity.

'Oh pooh,' one of them might say, 'who's gruffed?'
'It was Damian!'
'Was it you, Damian? Did you just grunty wunty?'
'Yes I did! Did you smell it?'
'Yes.'
'Tee hee!'
'Tee hee!'
No good to anybody, the Popper. Though it's just as well not to confuse it with its heavy leather counterpart, the Cruiser.

10. The Rattlesnake

Perfect for those occasions when time is against you, the Rattler slithers out with no warning, strikes, and slithers back.

Try to imagine a sort of low rasping sound in the key of A sharp, and that's your friendly neighbourhood Rattlesnake. You can round off a Rattler with a sustained final note, but in most circles this is considered a bit flash. Our only advice is to master the basic model before going for any of the bolt-on extras.

Aromatic content is not all it could be with the Rattler, so it's best used in places like fairly uncrowded restaurants, when your partner has gone to powder his/her nose. Do not unleash it under the wine waiter's nose, however. It could blur his judgement and spoil your whole evening.

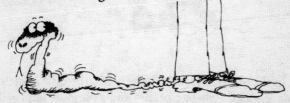

By the time your friend returns, our jolly little amphibian will have slinked off to cause damage and panic elsewhere. (You'll soon discover where, when you see ladies standing on their chairs and screaming.) If by mistake a little of the venom is left behind, simply blame it on the pasta that you've heard has just been pulled off the menu.

11. The Fisherman's Friend (or, the Grimsby Trawler)

Grim, delightfully grim. Downright lethal if performed correctly, the Fisherman's Friend makes for oceans of aroma, yet sounds like the merest slopping in the bilges.

It's a natural for those times when you want to put one down, but prefer to maintain your anonymity, e.g. when receiving a knighthood. And it's a real hot favourite with the ladies: catch a woman laying rubber and we'll lay you odds of a thousand to one that it's a good old Fishie, all the way from Marseilles.

In the olden days, this model used to be called 'Silent But Violent'. Change of diet and a national improvement in physical fitness have, however, brought about a few minor adjustments that justify the new title.

It's guaranteed to break the ice at parties, too, as you regale your fellow guests with stories about 'the one that got away'. But beware. You can't afford to burn your boats if you're thinking of starting a cod war.

12. The Bouncer

Put down a Bouncer and you'll get thrown out of anywhere. They do exactly as their name suggests, richocheting off the cornices and skirting boards, skidding dangerously out of control on washable vinyl.

They do make things go with a swing, though the sound of your head hitting the pavement as a result of getting caught isn't as much fun as it could be.

No matter how you dress a Bouncer up, they remain the same at heart – thick, pungent and objectionable. Treat Bouncers with respect and they will do likewise.

13. The Inter-City Sizzler

Forget the Bender on the 8.15 or the Away-Day Special – the Sizzler will get you from London to Newcastle and comes with automatic three-month return. But it's getting more and more expensive these days, so do save up as much washing powder as possible.

14. The Stun Grenade

A must for every arsenal, but probably best left to the SAS. Without proper training, it'll scare the shit out of you.

15. The Firecracker

Not, as you might at first think, a model restricted for military use. British Airways have given the same name to their early morning special to Inverness. It's absolutely first class, and British Midland can't do a thing to touch it.

16. The Volcano (in Moscow, the SS20)

If you're the kind of person that takes the bull by the horns, then this is the one for you. Acclaimed the world over as the grandaddy of them all, the Volcano is far and away our personal favourite, and should be the very pinnacle of your aspirations.

Tense? Nervous? Headache? Nothing acts faster than a really satisfying, rumbling, hearteningly resonant Volcano, and you'll be back there on cloud nine before you can say 'Vesuvius'. Express relief is just a Volcano away.

Volcanoes are a barrel load of laughs, but if they have one failing, it is their refusal to leave an aromatic calling card. For that reason, perhaps, they have not quite achieved the popularity you might expect with the more flamboyant of the cognoscenti. Still, you are always guaranteed comments like: 'You rascal you,' or, at sea, 'All hands to the pumps!'

You have our medical word for it that a Volcano will not do any lasting tissue damage to the nasal cavities of the receiver – it'll just sound as though it will . . .

17. The Dirty Old Toby

Also answers to the name of: the Barker, the Tiger, or Roll Over, Rover, and in Germany: der Englisher Schweinhund; in Australia: the Dead Dingo; and in Alaska: the Fusty Husky.

How many times have you heard those magical words 'You dirty dog' screamed in a public place?

Quite a few, with any luck.

Most authorities agree that the name derives from this rabid little chappie's unique olfactory coordinates: roughly mid-way between a Volcano and a Fisherman's Friend (and do we mean *roughly*), producing a fart that sounds like the bark of a scalded mongrel and smells like the bark of a very old tree.

Very definitely man's best friend.

18. The Perishing Missile

The ultimate deterrent. This is no joke, even the day after.

Forget the five-second warning – there won't be one. Greenham Common has proved that a bunch of wet farts are no competition for a nuclear blast, so don't press the button unless you have adequate shelter.

No wonder the Americans will be 3000 miles away when they deploy the damned thing.

2
The Way To A Man's Fart . . .

'There's no such thing as a free lunch.'
Johann Sebastian Bark

'A gastronomic blow out is a sure-fire winner'
The Poux Brothers

'An army marches on its stomach,' as Napoleon used to say. Or, when the Marquise de Pumpodour failed to supply him with enough of the old chicken'n'mushroom vol-au-vents to raise a decent mistral: 'Not tonight, Josephine.'

Now, as we already know from the Bender saga, breakfast is the most important meal of the day. But the body needs regular intakes of raw materials if it is to run at anywhere near full capacity.

Here, then, are your staple foodstuffs, and some recipes for your enjoyment. You will notice that we never mention hole food diets of arrowroot and yoghourt: such abuses of the digestory system cannot hope to hold a candle to a damned good feed of mushie peas and faggots. (N.B.: *Never* hold a candle to a damned good feed of mushie peas and faggots.)

1. Cold roast pork with chutney

Rustle up this little concoction and you're really nailing your colours to the mast. Never giving you less than one hundred per cent, the Pork'n'Chutney is one of the best double acts in the business.

Simply butter two thick slices of white bread, place on top of them a few slivers of choice roast pork (cold), smother generously with dollops of that mango chutney you bought on the WI stall at the local fête, put the bread together and eat it as fast as you can. Speed is everything with this one.

It's a real light-the-blue-touchpaper-and-stand-well-back job, this, at its most effective at about seven o'clock of a Sunday evening. Little do the people on 'Songs of Praise' realize how much support they're getting from us at home.

A decent-sized sandwich will last you right through the Sunday film, unless it's a Western – in which case you'll probably run out of ammo before the cavalry arrives.

2. Popcorn

Hog this down at huge speed, leave to ferment for thirty minutes during the film about New Zealand and the Pearl'n'Deans, and you'll stir up a hornet's nest every time.

The general outcome of popcorn is a Dirty Old Toby, but heaven knows why. Get a bucket load of it down your neck in the back row and it won't be just 'Earthquake' that you will be watching in sensurround.

3. Quarter pounder with large fries and vanilla shake

Once in a lifetime comes a combination of ingredients that captures the imagination of a whole generation. This is it. The Big One. Capable of producing more megatons of fall-out than even Einstein predicted.

We know someone who has actually evacuated half of Streatham at one time with this number (medical ethics prevent us from giving our patient's name, but we can tell you that it begins with Phil Puttock), and the police believe he could make a major contribution to crowd safety at Stamford Bridge.

One of the vilest recipes for success you'll ever lay your hands on, but handle it like sweating gelignite.

4. Sweetcorn or corn on the cob

Ever wondered why that Green Giant is so goddamned jolly? It's because the dirty bastard has spent the whole day laying Bouncers, that's why.

Just get hold of a whole corn on the cob and smother it with melted butter and WI mango chutney (if there's any left). Then walk the streets like a big, green, human time-bomb.

5. Baked beans

Never tried them.

6. Good old Christmas pudding

A firm favourite that has stood the test of time. The range of flavour and texture you'll get out of the stuff is frankly quite staggering.

When it's your turn to do your party piece you can take the stage with confidence, safe in the knowledge that you're sitting on close to ten cubic metres of Volcano. If not, we'll give you your money back.

Christmas pudding allows a most amusing variation, called the Klaxon. Best time to try one is when Grandad's out of it on the sofa. Creep up behind him and lay down a really full-blooded Klaxon – then watch the expression on his face as he runs for the shelter. But mind that the cunning old bugger doesn't light a match or you'll never hear 'The Sound of Music' again.

7. Guinness v lager

The true farter's dilemma. Everyone knows that Guinness is good for you, even if the occasional badly poured pint has been known to produce a Strangulated Toucan. On the other hand, a few pints of amber nectar down their necks has conjured up some of the vilest bouncers on earth.

So what's a man to do? Babycham, Perrier water or tomato juice will only result in serious popping, so stick to what you know will do the job. Only exceptions are Foster's lager for Australians, guaranteed to chuck out a few jet-propelled Boomerangs, and some of the better-named cocktails, like A Slow Comfortable Rattlesnake Against The Wall, or A Dirty Old Toby Between The Sheets.

8. And for dessert . . .

We would be grateful to hear reports from any of our readers (but not *too* loud, please) on the following unresearched foodstuffs: tinned custard; cold meat loaf; chocolate fudge brownies; potato waffles with golden syrup (out of the lion shall come forth . . . what?); cream eggs; avocado with prawns, wild duck paté; frozen cheesecake; tinned artichoke hearts.

Our cooking correspondent, Delia Sniff, would like to recommend the following for a light summer dish: onion sag with popperdoms; prawn crackers; frank-farters (you might know them as hot dogs), with bubble'n'squeak to follow – which it invariably will.

3
The Biggest Noises of All Time

> 'Bless 'em all . . . the long and the short and the tall . . .'
>
> *Percy Fysshe Smelley*

Well, we're certainly covering some ground, aren't we? Since you now know what to do and how to go about doing it, the time has come to identify some of your fellow farters – especially those whom we'd most-like-to-be.

In philosophy

Karl Popper ('The Open Society and its Enemies')

In the studio

Russell Farty

In the news

Angela Ripper

In the nude

Poo Stark

In high society

Fog – always thick and wet
Nigel Dumpster – always first with a whiff of scandal
Lady 'Bubbles' Rothermere

In high dudgeon

Grunter Davies

In troughs of low pressure

Michael Fish

In force ten gales

Edward Heath and the lads in Morning Cloud

In the clear

Blaster Bates
Dennis The Menace
Desperate Dan
Joan Bakewell

In the mists of time

The universally-acknowledged greatest fartsmith of all
time is Joseph Pujol (1857–1945), better known by his
stage name of *Le Petomane*.

Dr Marcel Baudouin, in his acclaimed tract, 'An
Extraordinary Case of Rectal Breathing and Musical

Anus' describes *Le Petomane*'s amazing ability to imitate all types of musical instrument from violin to trombone, and to sustain them for up to fifteen seconds. Pujol's famous Moulin Rouge stage act is described by his son: 'My father coolly began a series of small farts, naming each one. "This one is a little girl, this is the mother-in-law, this is the bride on her wedding night (very little) and the morning after (very loud). This is the mason (dry – no cement), this is the dressmaker tearing two yards of calico (this one lasted at least ten seconds and imitated to perfection the sound of material being torn), then a cannon (Gunners – stand by your guns! Ready, fire!), the noise of thunder, etc. etc."

'Then my father would disappear for a moment behind the scenes to insert the end of a rubber tube . . . it was about a yard long and he would take the other end in his fingers and in it place a cigarette which he lit. He would then smoke the cigarette as if it were in his mouth, the contraction of his muscles causing the cigarette to be drawn in and then the smoke blown out.

'Finally my father removed the cigarette and blew out the smoke he had taken in. He then placed a little flute with six stops in the end of the tube and played one or two little tunes such as "Le Roid Dagobett" and, of course, "Au Clair de la Lune".

'To end the act he removed the flute and then blew out several gas jets in the footlights with some force. Then he invited the audience to sing in chorus with him.'

4
Your Guide To Who Does What

1. The accountant

Never mind the double entry stuff, watch out for the double exit. He's a calculating swine, this one, in every sense. Guaranteed to pick the best possible place and time to put *you* on the spot. The accountant lets out banal Benders, turdifying Tobies and feeble Fisherman's Friends, shying away from the more demonstrative and flamboyant Volcano or Rattler on the grounds that they would ruin his reputation. Worst of all, he never carries the can. No wonder they're all stinking rich.

2. The journalist or 'news hound'

'Man bites dog' – and is it any wonder? Bleep Street is heaving with people like Linda Lee-Popper, George Gale and Janet Street-Pooter, theatre critics called Jack Stinker and metropolitan critics called John Gross.

They sniff out scoops, and revel in such by-line puffs as: 'The Man They Can't Gag', and 'The Column With The Sunday Punch'. Then they scream 'Gotcha!' when you cop a Printer's Devil hot off the press. No wonder it's called the Street of Shame.

3. The estate agent

Much more of a two up, two down Rattler, this chap.

He gets ever so excited when he's showing some prospective client around one of his crumbling 'des. res.'s' and his emotions sometimes get the better of him. It's probably got something to do with the thought of all your hard-earned semolians ending up in his manky little mitts. Enough to get the old cash registers a-ringing upstairs and the Rattlers a-rattling down below.

Yes, out comes the juicy Rattlesnake and 'Ha-ha!' he says, 'there's nothing like the sound of stripped pine floorboards creaking.' (And that was nothing like the sound of stripped pine floorboards creaking.)

4. The bank manager

If it's the Listening Bank, you're in luck. If not, hard cheese. Because if there's one thing this breed is more forthcoming with than advice on how to step up your repayments on that personal loan, it's a steady stream of Poppers and worse . . . underlining and punctuating his lecture with metronomic precision.

What can you do to retaliate?

Naff all, that's what. Making jokes about Saturday opening and calling him a sulphurous polecat is all very well, but it ain't going to get you the money you need for an engine rebuild on your Trans-Am.

5. The male hairdresser

There you are, encased in leatherette, your hair wringing wet after Adrian's administrations, your boat race in the mirror looking like death warmed up, when suddenly you hear that familiar little sound. Pop!

Who's a naughty boy then, Adrian? And you at his mercy, covered in a tent and towels and looking like an extra from 'The Poseidon Adventure'.

All you can do is glare at him meaningfully and watch him blush. The only drawback is that should he take it upon himself to throw a tantrum or bite through a grape or something, there's a good chance you'll emerge from his parlour looking like the last of the Mohicans.

Bit like we do at the moment, in fact.

6. The publisher

Many is the masterpiece we've pushed through this lot's letter-boxes, only to be told it needs a 'bit of tightening'. Even people you'd expect better of, like Corgi, or Dent, or Mills & Boom, manage only a few releases a week – and often those are in limp editions.

Present them with your runaway block-buster and they'll sit on it for months – then do everything they can to delay the launch.

Bunch of boring old Frankfarts, the lot of them. Best avoided.

7. The dentist

Any dentist that puts one down while you are strapped in that chair in his chamber of pain is a dogfondler of the first degree. Such fiendish tooth-pullers are mercifully rare, but they do exist. They send Dirty Old Toby out for walkies just as you're about to get the drill down your neck and there's not a damned thing you can do about it. It's not as if you could even grit your teeth – you have simply to lie there and suffer. Best advice is to pretend to yourself that it was you that did it, and try to seek some enjoyment that way.

8. The television person

Poofs! Pouffes! Pooves! Poofters!

Producers wear such tight white trousers they're impossible to grunt into, and the upshot is they have to carry their farts around with them in 'fun' briefcases (bought at the General Traffing Company).

How people who spend their whole days amid shouts of 'Cut!' and 'Roll them!', and a buzzing atmosphere of clapperboards and sound effects and gaffers, can end up such a feeble bunch of Poppers, we shall never fathom. No wonder there's so much overmanning – it takes twenty of them to lay a decent length of rubber . . . and twenty more to hold it.

Mind you, with pooters like Gerald Parper and Moira Blister floating around, perhaps you shouldn't be in such a hurry to write to Barry Toot and demand your licence money back.

What gets up our nose though, is the staging of so-called events like the Nationwide Pop Awards, fronted by Tony Bleakburn or Tony Wudda-Budda-Hodda-Watta-Botta-Gubba (see p. 56).

Only good person on television is Katie Boil, but only when fronting the 'Eurovision Fart Contest'.

9. The baby

Oochi-coochi-coo be damned. These small but perfectly formed dogfondlers can put down Fisherman's Friends, Boomerangs, Rattlesnakes and Bouncers with the best of them. Grown men have been reduced to weeping with envy at the sound and pungency of their offspring's efforts.

How the hell do they do it? It's not as if they're weaned on a diet of pork and chutney sandwiches and Big Macs with large fries, is it? If you've never seen a baby before, try going to a baby show. You could run half the cookers in England on the amount of gas that little lot are putting about.

(Kim came second at a baby show once. He never found out what for though.)

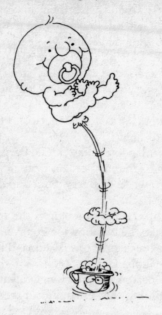

10. Man's best friend

When old Rover lets one fly (and you won't hear it, it'll just suddenly be there, like a gaseous version of the SAS), it's as vile as hell.

Little socialist that he is, Rover doesn't give a monkey's where he puts them down or who's around or anything. We mean, who else could fart in front of the vicar and get away with it? Not you or us, sister, that's for sure.

No, he's got it well sussed out, has old Rover. They say it's a dog's life, but we'd give anything to be old Rover sometimes.

11. The taxi driver

They're animals some of those cabbies. It must have something to do with them sitting around all day, their firing mechanisms vibrating away on the driver's seat. Working long hours means whipping into Macdonald's for a quick bite at lunchtime, and we know what that means. Catch a cab at about 4.30 in the afternoon and boy have you got problems. Now you know what those sliding glass partitions are for.

And why are those side windows always so goddamned hard to get down? They've got a great sense of humour, that's why. The only answer is to leave them with a Boomerang instead of a tip.

12. The sportsman

Walk into any changing room before a big game and you'll witness some fine examples of the noble art. There are the Poppers and Pre-match Jitters from the guys who are nervous about going out there on the turf, through to the Volcanoes and Up'n'Unders from those blokes that always strut around with their willies bouncing about.

As for the communal bath afterwards, you won't have seen such turbulence in the water since Jaws 2.

Some strapping examples of the men who are always trying to go faster, higher and longer are: Big Daddy, Hurricane Higgins, Guster Mottram, Peter de Savoury, Frank Boff, Brian Gruff, David Swine and Glen Wodda-Budda-Hodda-Wodda-Boddle-Hoddle (see pp. 56).

If you are of a sporting bent, all well and good, but our medical advice has to be that it is better to go for it in an upright position. Have a crack at ping-pong, the British Open or all-in wrestling (but only if you're confident of producing a submission with a Cross-Buttock).

As specialists, we are sometimes asked: 'Men admire my athletic prowess, but how do I bowl a maiden over?' The answer, of course, is to deliver a Bouncer, catch one in the slips, or, if you're called Iron Bottom or Fiery Fred, ask for middle and leg. Alternatively, try shouting 'Owzat?' at the moment of impact, or 'Fore!' if you're feeling particularly considerate, or 'It's the pits, man!' if you're just plain browned off.

There again, as Jockey Y-Fronts Wilson will tell you, a lot of women like you to go for a three-fart finish, whilst others will be content for you merely to raise chalk. As the saying goes, there's no accounting for taste: one of our patients, a famous London literary agent, insists on skiing with his legs wide apart at all times, despite our assurances that women do not inhabit the ditches he keeps falling into. It seems that for people like him, the call of duty is simply too great.

13. The horse rider

Talk about a watertight alibi! There's old Penelope Ffanbotham swanning about on Bluebell all day, dropping ffarts with a size and frequency that would take your breath away – and Bluebell's getting all the stick.

She'll knock out the judges at the three-day event.

14. The council worker

These fellows take some beating, and we wish someone would give it to them. How many times have you driven past a hole in the road when there are loads of pipes and things sticking out? Next time, stop and have a butcher's. You'll be greeted by about four great big fat Irish bums (they're upside down), the owners of which are stuffing themselves full of sausage sandwiches and Yorkies before laying down everything under the sun for the misery of the poor unsuspecting motorist. And they've got the nerve to blame it on a leaky gas pipe or the smell of hot tar.

DANGER MEN AT WORK

Best way to treat these people is to offer your views on why St Patrick was such a nurd for clearing Ireland of snakes, then get down that road like a bee's fart in a hurricane.

15. The granny

Strewth, some old grannies are more dangerous to life

and limb than a gang of glue-crazed muggers. Supermarkets, jumble sales, buses – these are their stamping grounds.

Brave is the man who helps an octogenarian rubber-burner across the road. No sooner have you grasped her arm than you're nuked by an antique weapon called the Darby'n'Joan. No wonder cars don't stop for them.

Mind you, grannies can get away with it because when all's said and done they're very sweet and kind and nice to children, and that's the way it should be. But have sympathy for the poor victim the next time you watch a mugging – the pooh-crazed youth who's had to run away, unable to withstand the onslaught from yet another granny who's 'had a go'.

One other point to remember: when you see a granny or old soldier in a pub, they'll invariably be drinking a half of bottled Guinness or Mackeson. The moral is clear. They may be older, but they're a lot wiser, too.

16. The postman

Now here's a bringer of bad news, if ever there was one.

Try this simple test next time your letters come tumbling happily through the box. Bend down, and inhale as your face approaches the ground. Notice anything?

Good old postie strikes again! He's just pushed one through your letterbox, hasn't he? First class. No wonder Rover's growling.

(Paperboys are also a potential source of danger, but they're far more likely to leave something on the step for you.)

17. You

Yes, what kind of person are *you*? And your friends? Simply decide the category you think you belong to, then turn over the page to check . . .

1. Vain ....
2. Amiable ....
3. Proud ....
4. Shy ....
5. Impudent ....
6. Scientific ....
7. Unfortunate ....

8. Nervous ....
9. Honest ....

10. Dishonest ....
11. Foolish ....
12. Thrifty ....
13. Antisocial ....
14. Strategic ....
15. Sadistic ....

16. Intellectual ....
17. Athletic ....
18. Miserable ....
19. Sensitive ....
20. Aquatic ....

. . . . One who loves the smell of his own fart
. . . . One who loves the smell of his friends' farts
. . . . One who considers his farts exceptionally pleasant
One who releases a Fisherman's Friend – then blushes
. . . . One who erupts a Volcano – then guffaws
. . . . One who farts a lot, on ecological grounds
. . . . . . One who tries awfully hard to fart, then follows
through
. . . . One who cuts himself off mid-fart
. . . . One who admits he's farted, but offers a good
medical reason
One who blames a Dirty Old Toby on dirty old Toby
. . . . One who suppresses a Rattlesnake for hours
. . . . One who always keeps a decent fart in reserve
One who excuses himself, then farts in utter privacy
. . . . One who conceals his farts with loud laughter
. . . . . . One who drops a Bouncer in bed, then fluffs the
covers over his mate
. . . One who can determine the perpetrator of any fart
. . . . One who can burn rubber at the slightest exertion
. . . . One who truly enjoys a good fart, but can't
. . . . One who dribbles out a Popper, then starts crying
. . . . . One who farts in the bath, then bursts the bubbles
with his toes

5
The Old Ones Are The Best

'We are not amused . . .'

Beatrix Popper

Laughter, as we fizzicians say, is the best medicine (apart from two weeks on a desert island with Hot Gossip). So here are some gags.

There was this bloke who simply loved baked beans and who simply loved the effect they had on him. There was nothing in his life that he enjoyed more than a good plate of beans followed by a really hefty fart.

He fell in love with a wonderful girl and eventually they married. All the time they spent courting, the bloke had lain off the beans and the farting, sacrificing both for the new love of his life. (The fool.)

Anyway, on the eve of his first anniversary, after a few drinks at the office with some of his mates, he decided he could not go on living without a plate of beans and a good fart. So on his way home he called in at an old café haunt and ordered the biggest plate of beans on toast you could imagine.

Feeling a whole lot better, he drove himself home and found his wife waiting for him at the front door with a blindfold in her hand.

'Hello darling,' she said. 'I want you to put this blindfold on as I have a surprise for you.'

She led him blindfolded into the dining room and sat him down at the table. 'I'll be back in a second,' she said, as she went into the kitchen.

God Almighty, the bloke thought. I've just eaten ten tons of beans and she's just cooked me a huge anniversary supper. There was only one thing to do to calm his nerves, and that was to let fly the most humongous fart he could. So he did, and if anybody had been timing it he would have won a prize.

His wife came back into the room and said, 'Darling, I have your surprise for you. You can take off your blindfold now.'

The bloke took off his blindfold and sure enough there was his wife with the most beautiful anniversary cake you could imagine. And there was his dining room table, and there were the ten dinner guests sitting round it . . .

There was a young man from Australia
Who parted his cheeks like a dahlia.
It went very well
At ten cents a smell
But a dollar a sniff was a failure.

Rich Outback

There was a young lass from Carshalton
Whose face had a big ugly wart on;
But to make up for that
She'd a great line in chat
And a fart like a 650 Norton.

Freda Rat

Burning question no.1

What do you call a fart in a trance?
Terry Wogan.

54

A young boy lets one out with his parents in the room.

'Timothy, how dare you do that in front of your mother!' the father shouts.

'Sorry, Dad,' replied Timothy, 'I didn't know it was her turn.'

The Queen was driving down the Mall with an important head of state when the horse pulling the royal carriage farted loudly. The Queen, extremely embarrassed, apologized profusely. 'Oh, I really am most frightfully sorry.'

Her Majesty's visitor turned to her and replied, 'That's quite all right, Ma'am, I thought it was the horse.'

And that is a true story . . .

A group of nuns are travelling on a corridorless train, and as the train stops at a station, a drunk lurches aboard and sits himself down.

A few miles down the track, he feels the call of Nature. A bit sheepishly he asks the Mother Superior if her nuns would mind awfully if he did it out of the window. 'Not at all,' she replies most charitably. So he relieves himself out of the carriage window.

A few miles on, he badly needs to go again. Again, he asks Mother Superior her permission. 'Not at all,' she replies once more, 'but this time, I think we'd prefer it if you peed in the carriage and sent your fart out of the window.'

Burning question no.2

What's the difference between a fart and a BMW?
None. Every arsehole gets one in the end.

There was an old major who had a faithful man-servant called Woddle. One night, the major decided to take his bath early and dismissed Woddle for the evening. Woddle bowed, and departed.

The major was just lowering himself into the steaming bath when suddenly there was a huge commotion of bubbles and froth as the old boy released one of his Vindaloo Avengers.

Minutes later, as the major was relaxing, there was a knock at the door, and in came Woddle. He presented his master with a hot-water bottle.

'Damn it, Woddle, what are you doing back? I thought I dismissed you for the evening?'

'So did I, sir,' said the manservant. 'But I was just going down the stairs when I distinctly heard you shout: "Oi, whod-abouda-hodda-wodda-boddle-Woddle?"'

The duchess was seated at the head of a long dining table, which was glittering with guests. Her footman was standing by her side. He coughed politely to signal that her ladyship was about to say grace, when barp! – the old girl let fly an enormous fart.

'John!' she shrieked. 'Kindly stop that!'

'Certainly ma'am,' the footman replied. 'Did you see which way it went?'

Burning question no.3

Why do farts smell?
For the benefit of the deaf.

Miss Smith asked her class to use the word 'definitely' in a sentence.

Little Lucy raised her hand. 'The sky is definitely blue.'

'That was a very good answer, dear, but the sky is

sometimes pink, or grey, too. "Definitely" has a stronger meaning.'

Jimmy raised his hand. 'The grass is definitely green.'

'Very good, Jimmy, but sometimes the grass is brown, or yellow.'

Little Tommy waved his hand.

'Yes?' said the teacher.

'Teacher, does a fart have lumps?'

The teacher was horrified. 'Tommy, what are you talking about? Of course not!'

'Well then,' said Tommy, 'I have *definitely* dumped in my pants!'

Burning question no.4

What is the connection between a soldier and a carthorse?
One darts into the fray, the other . . .

Mrs Berry was known for her Devonshire Bean Soup. When her secret for success was asked for, she replied that she used only 239 beans.

'How come only 239?'

'Because one more would make it too farty.'

On the first day of school, the teacher instructed her class on the correct way to get her attention if they had to go to the lavatory.

'Now boys and girls, if you wish to do Number One, raise one finger, and if you have to do Number Two, raise two. Does everybody understand?'

Everyone nodded.

About a week later, the teacher was startled to see Freddie frantically waving his hand.

'Why Freddie! What on earth is the matter?'

'Give me a number quick! I'm going to fart!'

Rhyming pong

A fart is a volcanic eruption,
It starts from the mountain called Bum;
It slides down the seat of your trousers,
And ends in a musical hum.

Roger McBoff

A cowboy in wild Oklahoma,
Had a bum that could sing 'La Paloma';
But his sweetness of pitch
Couldn't equal the hitch
Of impotence, size and aroma.

William Breakpeace Rattler

There was a young man from Newcastle,
Who had a collapsible arse'ole;
'Twas handy, you see,
When he farted at tea:
He could bend down and make up a parcel.

Paul McFartney

There was a young girl from Baia,
Who used to stick flutes up her rear;
After eating escargots
She could fart Handel's 'Largo' –
With an encore of 'Ave Maria'.

H.G. Smells

There was a young scholar from Stroud,
Who could fart unbelievably loud;
When he let go a big 'un
Dogs were deafened in Wigan –
And the windows fell out in the south.

Edgar Allan Pooh

The boy stood on the burning deck . . .

Pongfellow

6
Jane Dogfondler's Workout

'I must, I must, I must improve my thrust . . .'
Dorothy Parper

So much for the light relief. Now it's time to tune up the buttock muscles and clear out the tubes, and how better to do that than with a short, sharp burst of airobics?

(Readers are advised to consult their own doctor if there is any doubt as to their fitness to carry out the exercises illustrated.)

The boffin' coffin. A dead cert for a Dead Rat. This simple exercise will help you produce a fart that's good enough to be embalmed.

The tandoori squat. Really gets the sag (especially Onion Sag) out of your system.

The sweeper. Good defensive position, but keep an ear open for sliding tackles – unless you want to score the indescribably humiliating 'own goal'.

The stoker's mate. This is the one to clear out the clinker and keep you going full steam ahead.

The sergeant-major or, the horrible little man. Chest out, stomach in, by the left . . . wait for it, wait for it . . . quick . . . release!

The sooper dooper pooper scooper. If you're out to startle, surprise or impress, this exercise will have you doing some right old Bobby Dazzlers.

FART TWO
Coming Out

'Fart and the world farts with you.'
Vincent Van Bogh

Farting Zone's Law

A fart will expand to fill the space available.

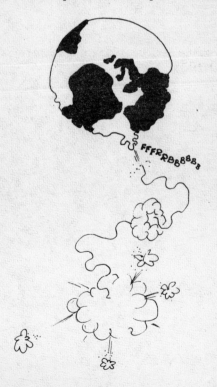

1
Dressed To Kill

'Farting is the most fun you can have with your
clothes on.'
                                    Hieronymus Boff

We are almost at the end of our Basic Training. Only
hours or even minutes now separate you from that
moment when, bursting with pride, you take your
rightful place in society as a fully-fledged farter and
member of BOFF.

Bear in mind that you are now also a black belt in
the martial farts, in charge of a highly-tuned and deadly
weapon: your lower digestory tract. Without discipline
and a keen self-awareness at all times, you could find
yourself lynched by vigilantes, recruited as a spokes-
man for the National Front, or coerced into appearing
on the Terry Wogan Show. (Don't say we didn't warn
you.)

But what are you going to wear? Not designer jeans,
we can tell you that right now. And not a frogman's
suit, either.

For full details of what this year's best-dressed farter
will be wearing – or not – simply read on.

1. Jeans

To be perfectly honest, a good pair of denims will never
let you down. Flexible enough to cope with virtually
every model, they're also tough enough to take the
strain for a decent length of time.

Favourites used to be baggy-arsed Wranglers, but hardened pros these days tend to go for Levi 501s. These strides are super-tough, with the added bonus of a not-too-tight fitting around the old firing line.

2. Designer jeans

It's obvious to us that Gloria Vanderbilt never did a fart in her life.

Designer jeans may be fab gear for Poppers, but that sort of antisocial behaviour isn't going to get you anywhere. Their 'sprayed on' characteristics leave no room for manoeuvre whatsoever – the most you'll get out of a pair of these thigh-grippers is a high-pitched whine, and that comes from your throat as you fight the anguish of a strangulated Rattlesnake.

3. Cords

As long as they're nice and baggy, you could do a lot worse than to opt for a fine pair of casual cords. Corduroy possesses a lovely deep rumbling quality, and you'll find as you go on that some of the world's greatest Volcanoes have erupted from beneath this most snobby of textiles and out through the green wellies.

4. Flimsy baggy trousers worn by actresses and academics

Not really on, sweetheart. No resistance you see – they're as limp as the wrists of the Poppers wearing them. The most you'll get out of these are a couple of half-hearted Tobies. Go for anything further up the Richter Scale and they'll billow out at the back, betraying your naughty secret to everyone else in the wine bar.

5. Racing drivers' suits

You have probably seen cases on television where a racing driver has had to leap from a blazing car as the result of an over-zealous Volcano, but mercifully such incidents are now very rare.

Fireproof material is a tremendous boon to professional drivers, enabling the emission of anything that takes their fancy. Le Mans is the best, they say, because the cars are enclosed and so lock in all the delicious aroma all the longer. What's more, the cars hurtle down the Mulsanne Straight at speeds well in excess of 200 mph – aided and abetted by many a Turbocharged Toby, we're sure.

6. Space suits

It is no accident – and certainly nothing to do with gravity – that astronauts are always floating up and down in the air. The explanation lies much closer to home: their suits are hermetically sealed, keeping dangerous radiation out and dangerous Rattlesnakes in.

We envy these brave men and women, but the moon's one hell of a long way to go for a bit of novelty bog-rocking.

7. Those long robes that archbishops wear

It's actually worth going to your local costume hire place and trying out one of these beauties, because they really are good news. Ventilation is second to none, and no one will suspect a member of the clergy of putting down that fetid Egg'n'Bacon Bender that brought the whole congregation to its knees.

Gets our blessing any time.

8. Mini-skirts and dresses

Utter Nirvana, the mini-skirt will enable you to demolish anyone, anywhere – except Lenin's Tomb and Moslem temples. Problem is, what self-respecting dogfondler is going to swan about in a mini-skirt or dress?

Answers on a postcard please, Timothy, to the usual address.

9. Kilts

What a brilliant piece of work the kilt is. Worn, of course, with no restrictive undergarments, this pleated attire will enhance the kill-zone of even the feeblest Popper.

If you possess the ability to go through the day with people calling you Jimmuh all over the place, then you're on to a winning streak with the famous 'Fartin' Tartan'.

In the various wars in which we banged away at the Germans, Scottish regiments came to be known as 'the devils in skirts'. It is our opinion that this is an inaccurate translation, the correct one being 'the devils that come from underneath the skirts', a reference surely to many a porridge-powered Volcano.

The Germans are such renowned Poppers, poor things. No wonder they've always come second.

10. Wet suits

Stay well clear of wet suits and never ever try to lay rubber when you're encased in rubber.

Jacques Cousteau once propelled himself at over forty knots across the surface of the Mediterranean after an unwitting Boomerang inflated his suit and made a break for it down his leggings.

2
Ongoing-for-it Situations

'What's a nice girl like you doing in a
place like this?'
'Fffiiissshhhh!'

There are moments in everyone's life when, like it or
not, circumstances demand that one does not release
the gorgeous Bouncer or Rattlesnake stored in the
breech.

Prima ballerinas know this moment well. So, too, do
some artists' models, Trappist monks, and hitch-hikers
with a false sense of decency. The Rattlesnake just has
to lie there coiled, while its owner grits his teeth, closes
his eyes, and dreams of being, say, a policeman on point
duty, or a cross-Channel swimmer.

So before we let you loose to go off around the
world, it is important that you learn the rudiments of
self-control in the following, easy-to-grasp, situations.

1. In an interview

Imagine the situation. You're seated opposite this old
geezer, answering questions, the interview's gone
down a bomb, and he's practically on the point of
asking you to marry his daughter, when . . . a certain
region of your anatomy suddenly sends the first signals
of appreciation for that fine breakfast you had exactly
four hours ago. Whaddya do?

Well, rule number one for interviews is that timing is
everything. Rule number two: only apply for a job at

smart, reputable companies. The rationale behind rule number two is simple. If it's a smart, reputable company, then the chances are that at the very moment you're wondering desperately what the hell to do with that Egg'n'Bacon Bender whose ETA can be measured in milliseconds, you are sitting on a very comfortable *leather* chair.

Leather, you'll remember with relief, can be coaxed into making a most familiar noise as you shift position. Not a million miles from the sound of our good friend the Rattlesnake, is it?

Okay, you've grasped the strategy. Now for the tactics. Remember, everything depends now on your ability to abort the launch of the Egg'n'Bacon Bender, and do the necessary mid-flight corrections to convert it into a nice leathery Rattler.

(a) Brace your upper thighs firmly on the seat and lean ever so slightly forward from the hips. This not only prepares you to deflect most of the blast backwards at an angle to the leather, but also alerts the engine-room to the fact that there is going to be a change of course.

(b) Still tensed, feet firmly on the ground, lift yourself a tiny fraction off the seat and tilt forward. You are now ready for the final part of this daring manoeuvre.

(c) Smile at your interviewer.

(d) Bringing your hand slowly up to your mouth, cough as if to clear your throat before speaking. In the same motion, smooth yourself back in the chair, taking care to maintain the angle of deflection at the rear, and release.

(e) Narrow your eyes almost imperceptibly to signal faint annoyance with the fabric of the chair. You may now cross your legs, and smoke if you wish.

It cannot be stressed too strongly here that the nature and standing of the company is all-important. If the job you're applying for is vaguely artistic and you're stuck in one of those low-slung chrome Italian things, with a release trajectory that cannot fail to spin the interviewer's wig through 180°, you may as well choose this as your moment to get up and give a noisy display of genius, or whatever it is they do to get jobs in places like advertising agencies.

Above all, remember at all times that you'll never seal the deal if the guy's writhing around on the floor in involuntary spasms.

2. On public transport

(c.f. THE FIRECRACKER, THE INTER-CITY SIZZLER, THE
INTER-CITY SLEEPER AND THE CHANNEL TUNNEL)

There are few joys as huge as laying down the rubber to
end all rubber, on a crowded bus, tube or train. It's
absolute bliss knowing that you're the rancid swine
that's put an entire carriage on the verge of upping
their cornflakes.

The trick here, and one that on all accounts must be
obeyed, is to keep a straight face. And we mean
straight. Not even a twinge, the faintest trace of a
smirk, or you're really in trouble and liable to a public
flogging. We know of many a professional who has
gone this route and come unstuck through lack of
discipline. Try to practise by laying down a few in front
of a couple of people at first, then build up gradually to
the ultimate carriage-load.

If you can pull off this merry stunt and live to tell the
tale, then you have the makings of a true champion.

3. In a lift

It's hard to think of times when you would *not* want to
burn a bit of rubber in a lift, though one might be when
the only two people in the lift are you and Bo Derek –
and the lift jams. Just for once, you'll probably have
more important things to discuss than the intricacies of
the perfect Bouncer. Shared body warmth to stave off
claustrophobia is as good an opener as any. At all other
times, of course, you'll be going for it in a lift as though
the noble art was going out of fashion.

Ever wondered why people in a lift are always
staring at the ceiling or at the little red lights that show
what floor you're coming to? They're trying to get
their noses as far away from the culprit's line of fire as

possible. If you get into a lift under these conditions, go for something with real guts to it, like a Boomerang, and teach the antisocial swines a lesson.

4. Dating

Never fart in the first five minutes of the first date. Rattlesnakes were not high on Don Juan's list of opening gambits. Juliet did not blow Romeo straight back off the balcony. James Bond would not have dreamt of rolling even the most dastardly Kremlin spy out of bed with a Dirty Old Octopussy. So don't you, either.

As the relationship progresses, and if your partner's a decent sort, then do by all means go for it – say, after ten minutes or so. You should find that it is put down to animal instincts, and that you are encouraged to do more. Try to preserve a *little* mystery, however.

As the relationship progresses further, see p. 78.

5. In the bath

Like solitary driving, farting in the bath is outrageously good fun. What a pity that recent so-called liberated views have led to shared baths; what you gain in companionship you sometimes lose in self-expression.

It is very important to learn a few of the ground rules of the bath. The first, as you might imagine, is to blow out the bubble bath. Bubble bath can lead to much confusion, although it has the compensation of providing the perfect smoke-screen to help you deny ownership of any particular underwater disturbance.

If you are bathing alone (well done) and your girlfriend/boyfriend/mum/wife/husband/social worker comes into the bathroom and hands you a hot-water bottle, you know you've been sussed out – but what a way to go!

If you don't understand what the hell a hot-water bottle has to do with anything, then refer at once to p. 56).

6. In the bookshop

How many times have you been at a loose end in one of these seats of learning, torn between Dante's *Inferno* and *Smelly's People*, when . . . your nostrils twitch, and . . .

yes . . . the loathsome Paperback Browser is upon you. Reeking of damp cardboard and remaindered copies of Jeffrey Archer books, its genre is hard to pin down – which is probably just as well.

But why just in bookshops? Nobody knows. Perhaps it's all that standing around amongst so much food for the brain. Or maybe it's all that sitting: the bookseller himself is certainly not above suspicion.

Best course of action when you feel one coming on is to run to the 'A' shelf of Fiction, grab any Jeffrey Archer book, and give vent to your criticism directly on to the printed page. Look around you and you will see at least ten other people doing the same.

Poor Jeffrey.

7. On the squash court

Strictly speaking, it's not very sportsman-like to traff on the squash court, but sometimes needs must.

If your opponent is wiping you off the floor, then you'll have no option but to wade in with a secret weapon – like a really decent Fisherman's Friend.

Best tactic is to lay one down when you're up at the front wall, then do a drop shot to force the other player up to the front wall and almost instant asphyxiation. Since squash is a game that relies on total concentation, there's nothing better than a choice cloud of mustard gas to scramble his brains. Leaving you to win the game and pick up a free pint of Guinness in the process.

Most games are open to manipulation in this fashion, but some, like football and cricket, can be a bit of a headache. It takes an all-out Iron Bottom to make any sort of impact on 100 square yards of park.

8. At a wedding

'I do.'

Well shame on you then, putting one down on such a meaningful occasion.

Actually, weddings are brilliant fun for the fartsmith.

Weddings can get so emotional and serious that there's really nothing for it but a couple of quick Rattlesnakes to sort the place out. Doesn't usually go down too well with the bride's mother but, what the hell, she's crying anyway.

Incidentally, if you're clever you can raise an absolute furore in the old church by laying down a few and glaring at the 'other side'. This snappy manoeuvre has probably broken up more happy occasions than you've laid hot Volcanoes. Do watch out for the flying vol-au-vents, however.

9. In bed

Magic. Anything goes. Give it the whole works. It's brilliant news.

Oh, you're sharing the bed with someone, are you? Oh. Not much we can say about that then. Right, well, one nice little technique that might get you out of trouble is to hold the sheets or duvet or newspapers or whatever, and gently fan them up and down – thereby expelling the aroma out the side. But it's the sort of waste that makes you ashamed to be called British.

More challenging, of course, is the cunning art of the side swipe. The side swipe must be executed almost as soon as you've released Dirty Old Toby, or it could lead to suffocation.

Simply lift the covers that are tucked into your side of the bed and fan away. If it's a duvet, you're laughing. (Unlike the poor family dog that's sleeping on the floor your side of the bed.)

If the side swipe doesn't work and your partner gets a load of your handiwork, then there's every chance they'll do a runner and spend the rest of the night on the sofa – or you will.

Whatever happens, you can't lose: you're back on your tod and free to go for it with gusto. No obstacles in your flightpath like legs, thighs and other bits. Just you and that poor bloody dog.

10. On the move

Driving alone is one of the finest pleasures on earth. Windows securely wound up, some humongous sounds occurring on the hi-fi and you can really go for it: Boomerangs, Bouncers, the whole shooting match.

There is, however, a cruel law of farting that states that the rankness of your latest Dirty Old Toby is in direct proportion to the likelihood of seeing the most beautiful hitch-hiker in the world, just yards after release. So much for laying some solitary rubber.

But what if you've got a back seat full of mother-in-law or if you've picked up that glamorous hitch-hiker *before* the discovery that you need to restore liberty to a few Fisherman's Friends?

Best way of getting out of this one is simply to pull in to one side of the road, mutter about tyre pressures, and get out to inspect the offending bits of car. But that's a blatant cop-out of course, and you know it. You're a true British traffer, and you enjoy a challenge. So what do you do?

Our advice is to go for either a Fisherman's Friend or a Dirty Old Toby. Anything else will be detected at once by its glorious tone, and the game will be up. Now head for the nearest bit of woodland, field, or anywhere with a bit of open ground that's grassed. Drive past it, release your trusty chum into the atmosphere, and im-

mediately start blaming the smell on the filthy horses or cows that just happen to be out of sight in that field over there. The whole trick is to get in your complaint *before* any other nostrils start twitching: attack is the best form of defence.

If you're in the middle of a city, your only chance is to find some roadworks pretty pronto and start moaning about leaking gas pipes. If not, or if you're stuck in a traffic jam, we can only suggest that you switch off the ignition, open your door, and run like hell.

If you want to burn some real rubber, mind you, you've got to get a decent set of hot wheels under you. Not just any old auto will do – remember, a car is a portable showcase for your finest works. Go for it in style.

In our experience, the up-and-coming dogfondler needs transport that is suited to his calling. The Hillman Avenger, for instance, is an admirable vehicle for the task in hand. So, too, is the Porsche Turbo, the Dodge Charger, the Plymouth Fury, the Austin Maxi or any Roller (but especially the Silver Cloud).

Don't be seen dead in the Mini, and keep a look-out for traff-ic cops and that fearsome beast, the Jealous Juggernaut (thus named because it's so envious of what's coming out of your exhaust system, it insists on a very close-quarters sniff – at 80 mph).

Open-top cars are useless for our purposes, and so are sun-roofs and convertibles. Encase yourself in solid steel and glass and you can't go far wrong (unless the damned thing has air conditioning, an air spoiler and high wind resistance). The more cautious among you may care to fit air brakes. We are convinced, too, that neck restaints against whiplash are a major contribution to farting safety.

And don't forget: think before you stink before you drive.

3
In And Out – A Guide To What's Done And Not Done

'Remember, at posh dinner parties, the fart must always be passed to the left . . .'

Barbara Fartland

We're there! Any minute now, you'll be ready for your very first outside broadcast.

One final section of advice still remains, however: a few words on the Ps and Qs of farting.

Out!

Under no circumstances whatsoever are you ever to put one down:

1. In space, where no one can hear you
2. During a Royal fartabout
3. During a 21-bum salute
4. Anywhere near any member of the Royal family
5. Except the corgis
6. In front of the vicar (unless your name is Toby)
7. In the bath if you've got a cold (waste of precious energy, leaning forwards for that little appreciative sniff)
8. When your best friend's giving you a piggy-back home because you're too wrecked to walk
9. When your tailor is checking which side you dress
10. When Cleo Rocus appears on the Kenny Everett Show (Hi, Cleo)

11. In a hot-air balloon (too much competition)
12. Near a doctor on call (you might confuse his bleeper)

In!

The rules allow – nay, demand – however, that you go for it:

1. In every cubic metre of the Labour Conference
2. In the reception area of Saatchi & Saatchi
3. In front of any Wimmin's Libber
4. Even if she insists it's her turn
5. In Chelsea wine bars
6. In any BMW
7. But twice in a 320 Series
8. On the cheque book of anyone earning over 25 thou
9. On any American Express Gold Card
10. On any letter from Access
11. In your boss's teacup
12. In your boss's ear
13. In both of Ken Livingstone's ears
14. Twice in both of any foreigner's ears
15. At a Barry Manilow concert
16. On the Barry Manilow album, cassette or souvenir programme of your choice
17. On the Terry Wogan of your choice

4
Going Off Around The World

> 'Rank dogs and Englishmen, go off in the midday
> sun . . .'
>
> *James Boffwell*

Sooner or later at this stage of your career, you're
going to get the urge to jet off around foreign parts, and
show off your new skills. This is normal, and nothing to
worry about. Lots of people do it. The Russians, for
example, go off from time to time and engulf places
like Hungary, Czechoslavakia and Afghanistan. Adolf
Hitler did a very famous rundfahrt in 1939 that
covered most of Europe. Another German, Henry
Kissinger, also put himself about a bit in the late
seventies, before being flushed out by Watergate –
Rattlesnake Diplomacy it was called.

You are no doubt wondering what our advice to you
will be, when you hear the call of the wild and find
yourself with itchy cheeks.

Well, remember that you travel not just as an
individual, but as an ambassador for this great country
of ours, and as a BOFF diplomat. So stick those CD plates
on your car (for Caution: Dogfondler), and display a
red placard that says: Plenty To Declare. Then it's up,
up and away, for a good bout of *farts sans frontières*.

There is only one way to go, of course. By air. Fly the
dogfondling flag from the moment you hit the
departure lounge, limbering up with two or three
really manky, fusty old Flying-Fisherman's Friends as

you cruise around the Duty Free shop. In our expert medical opinion, this is the only way you can safely acclimatize your body to the demands that will shortly be made of it at 20,000 feet.

Fly on a foreign airline if you can, preferably Lufthansa. This will enable you to start your missionary work that much sooner.

Demonstrate to your fellow passengers that ours was an empire on which the sun never set, but do be careful that there's nothing too inflammable in your line of fire. Amuse them, too, by releasing all the goodness of your in-flight meal – then ask those around you if they can come up with a suitable name for your new creation. If it's not appreciated, wrap it in clingfilm again and save it for later.

By the way, you might at some stage of the flight experience a strange popping noise in your ears. Don't be alarmed, it's only the steward.

Another mid-air possibility for the accomplished farter is that one of the air hostesses may invite you to join the Mile High Club. Again, no need for alarm. Simply follow her to the back of the aircraft, nestle down with her in the nearest galley, and trade Volcano for Volcano as best you can.

One final word of medical advice. You will hear the stewardess announce: 'Shortly after landing you will hear an increase in engine noise. This is due to reverse thrust and is standard procedure.' Rot! That noise is the combined effort of everyone on the flight deck doing their rendition of Germany's latest entry in the Eurovision Song Contest.

Back on *terra firma*, your immediate priority is to clear yourself a bit of space amongst the three million extras from 'Our Man in Havana' that are queuing up at Customs. For you, a cinch. Go up to the desk and say, 'Customs? Here's a British custom . . .' and as you utter the immortal words, introduce the ugly foreign bureaucrat to the intricacies of a well-laid Bender – you'll be through Customs in a jiffy, before you can say Guardia Civil.

Now you're on your own, free to roam as the whim takes you. As you drive to your hotel, try to convert the taxi-driver to your new-found way of life. Then, as you struggle the last kilometre or two on foot, keep your spirits up with thoughts of all that lovely ammo at the end of the rainbow. There is nothing to touch a nice bit of the old barbecued pork and Mexican rice, for example, for producing the kind of Dirty Old Torquemada that's so devastating it has the locals diving three hundred feet off the cliffs.

While abroad, you can hope for a spot of illness which can really extend your repertoire. Spanish Tummy is dynamite for Bouncers, but watch out for follow through – it doesn't look quite so good on the brochures. Delhi Belly is a real devil, producing the sort of nose-crumplers that even stop the sacred cows dead in their tracks. And Gyppy Tummy certainly puts you through your motions.

America is pretty good because of all the burgers and thick shakes. Do bear in mind, however (if you have one left after two days in Los Angeles), that in California you don't lay one down, you lay one back – but only in your own space, not someone else's (it just wouldn't be mellow). Unless, that is, you know where they are coming from themselves, which is probably off the wall.

Talking of walls, what about a blast down the autoburns of Germany, to see where our forefarters flattened Dresden? Stop at a bierkeller and watch those chaps in leather shorts slapping themselves all over as they try to shoo away a few unwanted Rattlers. Sink some lager and a bratwurst, bierwurst or Scharnhorst (we sank that one in 1942), then get the hell out as fast as your BMW will carry you.

Austria and Switzerland are pretty good as foreign places go, and you should definitely have a crack at firing a Bubbling Fondue or Dirty Old Heidi down an alpine horn if the offer is extended to you. You will be flabbergasted by the echo potential of the Swiss mountains: we went for the local speciality on the Matterhorn a few years ago – the Yodelling Toby – and the sweet thing is still running around above the snow line, apparently trying to catch its own tail.

Elsewhere in Europe, our hottest recommendations are Denmark, home of the Danish Pastry (light and fluffy); Italy, home of the Spag Bol Surprise (it keeps trying to retreat); and Belgium, home of that wonderful attraction, the Manikin Piss-and-follow-through.

Which brings us last, but very much not least in terms of the bomb-load we carry when visiting it, to France. France, that seat of the arts since well before our beloved Nelson fell at Traff-algar. France, where they even wrote of '*F'art pour f'art*' and went on to invent that dramatic new delivery technique, the French Revolution. (When told that there was no bread in Paris for the peasants to make their pork'n'chutney sandwiches with, Marie Antoinette retorted: 'Let them cut cake'. Not bad, considering it would be at least another 150 years before anyone in Britain turned the other cheek with that worst of all ready-baked farts, the Mr Kipling French Fancy.)

France. It really takes some beating as a target, doesn't it? No shortage of fodder, mind you (unless you specially wanted English lamb). A quick stroll down the *Champs Elysees* after a plateful of *coq au vin* and *escargots* will soon have the old frogs hopping all over the place, screaming: '*Le bosche revient! Le bosche revient!*'

(Terribly satisfying, but beware of going for it within twenty metres of the Eternal Flame.)

Essential items for the journey
The Inter-City Sizzler
The Jumbo
The Flying Scotsman
The South Circular

How to make sure they get your drift
(Suivez le fiiisssshhhh!)

English:	*There's plenty more where that came from.*
French:	*Apres moi, le deluge.*
German:	*For you ze war is over.*

English:	*Geronimo!*
French:	*Vive la France!*
German:	*Achtung, Englander!*

English:	*I'm sorry, how can I ever make it up to you?*
French:	*Voulvez-vous m'accompagner au danse ce soir?*
German:	*I vas only obeying orders.*

FART THREE
Higher And Higher

'If I have farted further, it is by standing on the shoulders of giants.'

Isaac Megaton

Soon there'll be no stopping you.

In just a few pages from now, you will be ready to leave our clinic. We shall say: 'Off you go, you dirty dog.' And, beaming with pride, you will launch yourself into a future that holds nothing but promise, black looks and attempts on your life.

You will truly be On Your Own. Farting solo, no longer under our protective wing.

Heed, therefore, our final pearls of wisdom on how to relax, and how, in time, to set your sights higher.

1
Some Books To Get Your Nose Into

The best-smeller list

1. *Ten Days That Shook The World*
2. *Fair Stood The Wind For France*
3. *The Way The Wind Blows* (by Sir Alec Douglas-Fume)
4. *Dirty Harry*
5. *Slaughterhouse 5*
6. *Brief Candles*
7. *Is Paris Burning?*
8. *Coming Up For Air*
9. *She Stoops To Conker*
10. *Clinging To The Wreckage*

(Also doing well: *Sid Farter* by Hermann Hiss, and *The Fart Pavilions*)

New releases

The Earth Moved by Barbara Fartland (pub. Mills & Boom)

Whatever will Miss Fartland come out with next? Crammed with more cads, stinkers and girls getting the vapours than we've seen since *Jane Air*.

Strewth by Anthony Traffer (pub. Phewtura)

An explosion shatters the peace at Boffers, country seat of Lord Popforth. Whodunnit? Was it the butler? Or

JOIN THE RANKS
by Major Breakthrough

Are you ready for the cut and thrust of modern warfare? If your back was against the wall, could you achieve a breakthrough and go all out for victory? Do you understand the implications of a pincer movement, shock tactics and dive-bombing?

What *is* a flying column? A glider? A ground-to-air missile?

Are you trigger happy? Do you believe in biological warfare? Would you ever go near a foxhole, or would it depend on what the fox had been eating?

If you know the answers, then welcome to the Desert Rats – or if you prefer, the Special Air Service (motto: Who Dares Winds).

You are now ready to handle a Bouncing Bomb, Bangalore Torpedo, Bazooka or Flamethrower, and to star in 'The Great Escape', 'All Quiet On The Western Front' or 'Force Ten From Navarone'.

You are ready to utter such immortal phrases as: 'Halt! Who goes there?' 'Strewth!! Who yomped?' and 'I counted them all out, and I counted them all back.'

Welcome to the Air Force. You are indeed a professional.

the vindaloo? A real sniff-hanger, that beats the pants off Smellery Queen.

The Fart Report by Erica Pong (pub. Women Against Cutting The Cake)

By the authoress of *Fear Of Farting*, this book is like a breath of fresh air on the feminist scene.

OUT NOW
THE 1984 GOOD FART GUIDE

How to pump a good pint of Old Peculiar, Winter Warmer, Dog Bolter and Toby Bitter.

Only Heineken can do this, because Heineken refreshes the farts other beers cannot reach.

Issued by CAMRA: Campaign For Real Air

2
Pooh-It-Yourself

'Give us the tools and we will finish the job.'
Nostradanus

1. The oldest trick in the book. If ever, for some extraordinary reason, you should want to disguise the full wondrous aroma of one of your efforts, simply light a match and hold it burning until the smell of scorched flesh takes over. That's your fingers, and the room should now be clear of fumes.

2. Talking of matches, we all know the joy and pleasure to be gained from literally burning our rubber as it emerges. Lie on your back, legs well out of the firing line, and get a friend or acquaintance (or the chap you met ten minutes ago in the Chelsea wine bar) to hold a lighted match near to the source of the leak.

Best performed in total darkness, and bare-bummed – going for it through denim or any other fabric tends to produce a diffused 'simmering' level of flame that's no use to anyone.

Scratch'n'sniff
Scratch your thumbnail inside this box whilst laying down a Volcano, and sniff:

Burn by numbers

WARNING TO PERSONS OVER THE AGE OF 18:
it's best to get mummy to help you with this one.

Holding this page approximately six inches from your flame-thrower, follow the code to see what to put where.

1. POPPER
2. VOLCANO
3. RATTLESNAKE
4. EGG'N'BACON BENDER
5. BOOMERANG
6. FISHERMAN'S FRIEND
7. BOUNCER

Another whacky ruse is the old schoolboy's farting machine illustrated here. Simply bend some coat-hanger wire to the shape shown, put a washer in place with strong rubber bands, then wind it up and sit on it. To release a naughty noise, simply raise one buttock and watch auntie's dentures fall into the soup.

The old schoolboy trick

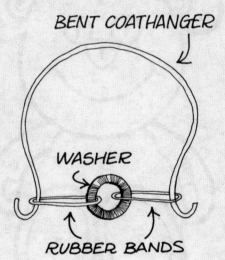

BENT COATHANGER

WASHER

RUBBER BANDS

3
What's On The Air Tonight?

(Now put your feet up in front of the telly.)

Channel F

('I never knew there was so much in it.')

7.00   FART TO FART

8.00   DULLARSE
More foul goings-on at Southpork, with Pooh
Ellen, Miss Smellie, Bobby Popper and Sniff
Barnes. In tonight's episode, JR smells a rat, and
the Poisoned Dwarf looks guilty.

9.00   ADULT MOVIE:
'One Flew Over The Cuckoo's Nest'

FFTHHBBBB

10.00   NOT THE
NINE O'CLOCK
POOHS
with Smell
Sniff and Gruff
Rhys-Jones

10.30   THE WINDS OF
WAR (repeat)

12.00 I FART ON YOUR GRAVE
(A video nasty)

ON RADIO, there's 'Call My Gruff', the 'Capital Fart-in', and 'Does The Panel Stink?' Classical fans might prefer to tune to Radio 3, where they can listen to *Wagner's Ring*.

There now follows a commercial break . . .
(If you've got it, flaunt it)

HEINEKEN REFRESHES THE FARTS OTHER BEERS CANNOT REACH

KEEP 'EM FLYING
(WWII slogan in support of
the US Air Force)

IN SPACE NO ONE CAN HEAR YOU LAY RUBBER

THE BEST TO YOU EACH MORNING
(fine slogan for Egg'n'Bacon Benders)

IT'S SO BRACING

LET THE TRAIN TAKE THE STRAIN

SNAP! CRACKLE! POP!

IS SHE . . . OR ISN'T SHE?

AT SIXTY MILES AN HOUR THE LOUDEST NOISE IN THIS NEW ROLLS ROYCE COMES FROM THE DRIVER

WHERE THE RUBBER MEETS THE ROAD
(Firestone tyres 1976)

IT'S THE REAL THING

LIPSMACKINTHIRSTQUENCHINACETASTIN
MOTIVATINGOODBUZZINCOOLTALKINHIGH

WALKINFASTLIVINEVERGIVINCOOLFIZZIN. . .
DIRTY OLD TOBY

SCHHH . . . YOU KNOW WHO

DESPERATION. PACIFICATION.
EXPECTATION. ACCLAMATION.
REALIZATION.

AND ALL BECAUSE THE LADY LOVES . . .
AN EGG'N'BACON BENDER

FULL OF EASTERN PROMISE

A VOLCANO GIVES A MEAL MAN-APPEAL

THINGS HAPPEN AFTER A BADEDAS BATH

ANY TIME, ANY PLACE, ANYWHERE

EVERY BUBBLE'S PASSED ITS FIZZICAL

A FART A DAY HELPS YOU WORK, REST
AND PLAY

JOHNNY WALKER: STILL GOING STRONG

TEACHER'S: A WELCOME AWAITING

BELL'S: AFORE YE GO

IT'S A LOT LESS BOVVER WITH A HOVVER

We now interrupt this chapter to bring you an important broadcast from Scotland Fart.

Not guilty

'Et tu, Brute?' *Julius Seizure*

Readers are asked to keep a look-out for the following offenders: the Boston Strangler, the Yorkshire Ripper, the Phantom Of The Opera. All are real killers, and you should not attempt to approach them. They may be armed.

Luckily the Flying Squad, the Filth, the Fuzz and several van-loads of sniffer dogs are on the scent.

If you'd like to 'have a go', make sure you learn one of the martial farts, like Kung Pooh or Pudo. One or more of these phrases may come in handy when you're grilling your suspect: 'Alimentary my dear Watson' or 'Stand and deliver' or 'Will you come quietly?'

If you'd rather not get involved with real-life Pops and Rubbers, try these from the safety and comfort of your armchair: 'No Hiding Place', 'Softly, Softly', 'Bravo, Juliet!' or 'Pumphole of the Bailey'.

If going straight is too much for you, you'll win our undying admiration for committing either or both of our favourite crimes: disturbing the peace, and setting fire to one of Her Majesty's dockyards.

4
The Pop Scene

Hi, pop pickers! This is Stewpot, Fluff and the Hairy
Monster welcoming you to the world of heavy sounds
. . . so just strap the Sony Fartman back on your head,
and cum on, feel the noize . . .

Fave 'Top of the Poppers'

Sid Vicious
Johnny Rotten
Buck's Fizz
Bad Company
The Pretenders
Men At Work
Dire Straits
Captain B. Fart
Dexy's Midnight Runners
Andrew Laid-Rubber

Flavours Of The Month
(Compiled by courtesy of *Sounds* and *Melody Maker*)
The Headbanger
The Body-Popper
The Demo
The Middle-Of-The-Road
The Ghetto Blaster (the rankest form of rastafart
that'll ever greet the nostrils)

Top of the Pops
(Including some all-time 'Blasts From The Past')

WE GOTTA GET OUT OF THIS PLACE	The Animals
POP! GO THE WORKERS	The Barren Nights
GOOD VIBRATIONS	Beach Boys
WE CAN WORK IT OUT	The Beatles
IT MUST BE HIM	Vicki Carr
BANG BANG	Cher
BOOM, BOOM, OUT GO THE LIGHTS	Pat Travis
NICE ONE, CYRIL	Cockerel Chorus
DIDN'T I BLOW YOUR MIND THIS TIME	The Delfonics
SOME KINDA EARTHQUAKE	Duane Eddy
DON'T BLAME ME	The Everly Brothers
KILLING ME SOFTLY	Roberta Flak
I'VE GOT YOU UNDER MY SKIN	Four Seasons
IT'S NOW OR NEVER	Elvis Presley
NOT FADE AWAY	Rolling Stones
SURRENDER	Diana Ross
BLOWIN' IN THE WIND	Donovan
SOMETHING IN THE AIR	Thunderclap Newman
BLOCKBUSTER	Sweet
CUM ON FEEL THE NOIZE	Slade
I HEAR YOU KNOCKING	Dave Edmunds
DISTANT DRUMS	Jim Reeves
RELEASE ME	Englebert Humperstinck
SILENCE IS GOLDEN	The Tremeloes
GET OFF OF MY CLOUD	Rolling Stones
ALWAYS SOMETHING THERE TO REMIND ME	Sandie Shaw
RETURN TO SENDER	Elvis Presley
SMOKE GETS IN YOUR EYES	The Blatters
ALL SHOOK UP	Elvis Presley

WHATEVER GETS YOU THROUGH THE NIGHT	John Lennon
CRACKLIN' ROSIE	Neil Diamond
ONE BAD APPLE	The Osmonds
LIGHT MY FIRE	The Doors
TIGHTEN UP	Archie Bell & The Drells
STOP! IN THE NAME OF LOVE	The Supremes
I CAN'T HELP MYSELF	Four Pops
MEMORIES ARE MADE OF THIS	Dean Fartin'
I HEARD IT THROUGH THE GRAPEVINE	Marvin Gaye
GLAD ALL OVER	Dave Clark Five
HONEY, COME BACK	Glen Campbell
I MAY NEVER PASS THIS WAY AGAIN	Perry Coma

5
Coming Your Way Soon. . .

May we remind you that for the comfort of patrons who prefer not to fart, the right-hand side of this cinema has been designated a No Farting area.

Far-from-silent movies

THE SOUND OF MUSIC	starring Julie Andrews Liver Salts and Christopher Bummer
SWEET SMELL OF SUCCESS	with Marlon Pongo
IT HAPPENED ONE NIGHT	with Dirk Bog-rocker
THE TROUBLE WITH HARRY	starring Cary Grunt
GONE WITH THE WIND	starring Atlanta, the city that burned

THE DIRTY DOZEN	starring Blurt Reynolds
BLOW UP	featuring Pat Boom, with special gust appearance by Perry Coma
HELLZAPOPPIN	starring Dean Fartin' and Ellen Burstin'
BREATHLESS	with Montgomery Whiffed
NORTHWEST PASSAGE	with Rip Torn
THE STING	with Dyan Cannon
CLOSE ENCOUNTERS	with Thrustin' Boffman
SOME LIKE IT HOT	including Katharine Hipburn
THE EGG & I	starring Lillian Gush
REVENGE OF THE PINK PANTHER	with Peter Smellers

Powerful moments of the silver screen

'You ain't heard nothing yet.'
Al Jolson in 'The Jazz Singer' (1927)
(The first words ever uttered in a talkie.)

'Listen to them . . . creatures of the night. What music they make!'
Bela Lugosi in 'Dracula' (1930)

'I never dreamed that any mere physical experience could be so stimulating . . .'
Katherine Hepburn to Humphrey Bogart in 'The African Queen' (1951)

'I want to be alone.'
Greta Garbo

'You dirty rat.'
James Cagney

On stage

'It'll all be all right on opening night.'
Sarah Burnhard

NOISES OFF and STEAMIN' by Nell Dung

BEDROOM FARTS and PLENTY by Alan Acheburn

THE REAL THING, WHODUNNIT? and MURDER AT THE VICARAGE by Peter Traffer

ENEMY OF THE PEOPLE, INADMISSIBLE EVIDENCE and A BEQUEST TO THE NATION by Terence Ratagain

THE LADY'S NOT FOR BURNING by Christopher Fry
DIRTY LINEN by Tom Boffhard

Some great spoutings forth

1. Is this a dogfondler I see before me?

2. I came, I saw, I conkered . . .

3. I wandered lonely as a cloud . . .

4. If you can drop Volcanoes when all around you are merely putting down Poppers . . .

5. Desiderfarta: Go flacidly amid the noise and haste . . .

6. 'Tis a far better fart I do, than I have ever done . . .

7. Romeo, Romeo, wherefore fart thou, Romeo?

8. To beep or not to beep . . .

9. Tiger, tiger, burning bright . . .

6
From Cradle To Grave

Henry VIII rocked many a banquet in his time. So he knew what he was talking about when he penned this riddle:

What is it that being born without life, head, lip or eye, yet doth run roaring through the world till it die?

Answer, of course, a fart.

But His Majesty was wrong about one thing. A fart doesn't die, it roars through the world for ever. For matter cannot be destroyed, it is merely recycled. So with every breath you take, the poor old lungs are taking on board up to twenty manky molecules left behind by such famous forefarters as Henry VIII himself (enough to take your head off), Benito Mussolini (lacking in character, but frequent and on time), or even Adolf Hitler (the Final Solution).

So now you know, for example, what that snake was doing in the Garden of Eden. And to help you even further, there now follow a few other facts you need to know about life's long, dark passage – from delivery, till death do us fart.

Midwhiffery

Thanks to the trail-blazing efforts of Le Boyer and others, delivery need no longer be a harrowing experience.

Start breathing classes as soon as possible, and learn

111

how to recognize a contraction, and when to push. Learn, too, the symptoms of sympathetic farting that occur in some husbands.

In the labour ward, we warmly recommend gas and air. Don't be bullied into lying on your bed with your legs in stirrups: feel free to walk around, or adopt any position that feels comfortable. In France, the woman often lies in a warm bath, with candles burning. Both of these things can provide much entertainment in their own right.

Only in extreme cases is there any call these days for the forceps. Stitches are even rarer.

Flying the nest

You will derive much pride and pleasure from all of the following:

The Toddler.

The Conker. (Used competitively in school playgrounds. The unofficial British champion is believed to be a ninety-niner – the rank swine.)

The Stinker. (Sets in at adolescence, and may hang around the house for as long as another ten years.)

Some things we wish we'd known at 18

One man's meat is another man's poison.

Early to bed, early to rise,
Makes your duvet reach for the skies.

History repeats itself.

Old soldiers' never die, they simply fade away.

Walls have ears.

Revenge is sweet.

Worse things happen at sea.

The end justifies the means.

The best things in life are free.

There's more than one way to skin a cat.

He who farts last farts the longest.

One thing we're glad we didn't know at 18

A twenty-six-year-old Dane died on the operating table when an electrically heated surgical knife caused his stomach to explode. Dr Niels Olsen, the surgeon, said the knife had burned through the patient's digestive tract and ignited explosive gases. The explosion was so violent that part of the colon was completely destroyed. In spite of further operations to repair the damage, the patient died of blood poisoning.

Maxims for happier farting

1. Never put off till tomorrow, that which you can put down today.
2. If in doubt, let it out.
3. A rip-stitch in time saves nine.
4. Go for it.
5. Do unto others as you would have them do unto

THE FARTER'S CREED

Greater love hath no man, than that he lay
one down for his friends.

---

6. Actions speak louder than words.
7. All's fair in love and war.
8. The bigger they come, the harder they fall.

9. Variety's the spice of life.
10. As you bake your bed, so must you lie on it.
11. Beauty is in the eye of the inhaler.
12. If at first you don't succeed, try a quarter pounder with large fries.
13. A bad workman always blames his stools.
14. Every cloud has a silver lining.
15. He who buys the curry calls the tune.
16. If Mohammed will not come to the volcano, then the volcano must come to Mohammed.
17. There's none so deaf as those that will not hear.
18. You can't make an Egg'n'Bacon Bender without breaking eggs.
19. Practice makes perfect.
20. A Fisherman's Friend in need is a friend indeed.
21. Strike while the iron is hot.

Some myths that need exploding

Small is beautiful.

Silence is golden.

Three's a crowd.

Less is more.

Empty vessels make the most noise.

A blurt in the hand is worth two in the bush.

Always save something for a rainy day.

Look before you beep.

A little burning is a dangerous thing.

Famous last farts

'Tirez le rideau, la farce est jouée.'
(Bring down the curtain, the fart is played.)

Ivor Taper

'I think I have eaten one of Bellamy's veal pies.'

William Pitts

'Thank God I have done my duty.'

Horatio Smelson

'We shall this day light such a candle . . . as I trust shall never be put out.'

Sir Francis Snake

'I am just going outside, and may be some time.'

General Guster

'More light, more light!'

Picarso

7
What Uranus Holds In Store

A dogfondler's guide to the galaxy

Aries
The first fire sign. (Get out the Swan Vestas, Mum.)

You're full of drive and energy, chasing new ideas and means of self-expression, often coming out with something quite stunning. You *love* to give yourself an airing amongst friends.

Taurus
The sign of the producer. (Often musical.)

Let it all hang out, Taurus. You're holding back, and this is stopping people's enjoyment of you. Beneath that smokescreen lurks a deeply romantic streak – find a partner with a boxer dog and go for it.

Gemini
The first air sign. (Well done.)

Your life is devoted to making everything around you more riveting and beautiful. The need to influence those around you means you are seldom silent. Good for you, Gemini.

Cancer
The first water sign. (Get the hot-water bottles out.)

Infinitely adaptable and patient, you are a jack of all farts – master of phew. You have it within you to make others feel ecstasy, sorrow, joy and compassion. You love an audience. (Famous Cancerians: Susanna Pork, Judi Stench, Peter Bowels, Farrah Force-it, Fart Garfunkel.)

Leo
Sign of the top dog.

You cannot fail to leave your mark on people. Everything about you is warm and friendly (roll over, Rover). You love the finer things in life, like burning rubber down your partner's legs as you lie encased in black satin sheets.

Virgo
Ruler of the abdomen and intestines. (Good news, Virgo.)

You have a strong desire to devote yourself to the service of others. You are the supportive one in the background, saying 'Well done!' and 'What do you do for an encore?'

Libra
Sign of good balance (between sound and aroma).

You have a splendid nose for injustice, which you blast off the earth whenever you sniff it out. You're full of fun, too, which means your trousers are full of burn holes from entertaining the kids.

Scorpio
Sign of the perfectionist.

You put them down in a clear and distinctive manner. You strive for self-improvement, but must beware of the sting in your own tail. You're never outnumbered in a Chelsea wine bar.

Sagittarius
Sign of the sage. (With onions, a sure-fire winner.)

You just love getting to the bottom of things. You can be guilty of lack of consideration for others, though, and you have a tendency to turn your nose up at the rubber your friends are so proudly burning. Poor show Sagittarius.

Capricorn
Sign of the prober.

You know how to be frugal and thrifty without appearing the least bit mean; with even the tiniest Fiiissshhh! you could feed five thousand. Your dogged efforts will take you steadily upwards.

Aquarius
Another air sign. (Can't have enough of them.)

You're a bit of a polyglot on the quiet (and not so quiet), often going wherever the wind blows you. Lots of loyal companions, as they quickly realize that anything can happen when you're around.

Pisces
The fish.

Say no more!

8
The Agony Column

Not in tune with the eighties? Partner getting up your nose?

Don't bottle it up. Get it off your chest, bring it all out into the open.

Dear Marje Poops
Every time I burn rubber in front of my boyfriend, my ankles swell up. What should I do?

Take off your tights.

Dear Marje Poots
People keep calling me a boring old fart. How can I make my farts funnier?

Send them to Jasper Carrott.

Dear Marje Toots
I put down a Dirty Old Toby in bed last week and it's still there. My husband refuses to sleep with me. How can I keep it there till Christmas?

Let sleeping dogs lie.

Dear Marje Hootsmon
I think this book stinks.
Choked of Edinburgh.

Where's your sense of humour, Choked? Oh sorry, I didn't notice that you come from Edinburgh.

Dear Irma Blurtz

Last Sunday my girlfriend took me down to meet her Mummy and Daddy at their mansion in Wisborough Green in Sussex. I was nervous, and had hardly got the first slice of pork down my throat when this tiny little fart made a bolt for it.

'Winston!' shouted Mummy, at the family dog that was lying at my feet.

I was so relieved to be let off the hook, that I let fly something with a bit more guts to it.

'Winston!' my future mother-in-law called sharply.

I thought to myself: I've got it made. One more and I'll have room for the plum crumble. So I burned enough rubber to make a major contribution to nasal safety.

'Winston!!' shrieked the ex-mother-in-law. 'Get over here before that schmuck dumps on you!'

What can I do?

I think you've done it all already. Just make sure it's Golders Green *next time, Foul Bowels.*

The farts expressed in this column are not necessarily those of the editor.

9
Aftermath: Where Do We Go From Here?

Well, have you passed?

Have those around you passed out?

Can you say with a clear conscience: today I have reached into myself, and I have come up with the goods. Much was demanded of me, and much is what I have provided. I have delivered. I am, in short, the rancid swine I set out to be.

Now, and every waking moment of your life, you must endeavour to live by the motto that we all hold so dear: Stink Big. And though you will by now realize that farting is one per cent inspiration and ninety-nine per cent perspiration, you must never cease to practise the noble art, to defend it against its detractors, to strive to bring it to its rightful place in the world: as an Olympic sport, by which the standard for all of us shall be set.

If you undertake these things, then well done, it was a pleasure doing business with you, and we are glad to welcome you to the fold.

For your free Ph.D (Doctor of Pharting, just like us – you see, we're not real doctors), simply put the correct name against each of the quotations below:

(a) 'I stink, therefore I am.'   1. Napoleon Bonafarte
(b) 'Hell is other people.'   2. René Desfartes
(c) 'J'accuse.'   3. Jean-Paul Fartre

Then fart along the dotted line, and send your entries in a large, airtight jar to: M. Mitterand, Elysees Palace, Paris, France.

10
Poohs Flash

It has been brought to our attention that two eminent herbal doctors have come up with 'cures' for farting. F and V Mitton go for a mixture of gentian, calamus, blackthorn, peppermint and camomile. Professor Hans Flueck, however, prefers caraway, fennel, peppermint, garlic, ramsons, yarrow and alpine mugwort.

Cures?!! What *do* they think they are playing at?

*On the following pages are details of Arrow
books that will be of interest.*

THE DIETER'S GUIDE TO WEIGHT LOSS DURING SEX

Richard Smith

Tired? Listless? Overweight? Open this book at any page and discover everything you wanted to know about sex, food and dieting but never dreamt of asking.

Activity	Calories burned
REMOVING CLOTHES	
With partner's consent	12
Without partner's consent	187
Unhooking bra	
Using two calm hands	7
Using one trembling hand	96
EMBARRASSMENT	
Large juice stain on shorts	10
ORGASM	
Real	27
Faked	160

(Continued on page 81)

BESTSELLING HUMOUR BOOKS
FROM ARROW

All these books are available from your bookshop or news-agent or you can order them direct. Just tick the titles you require and complete the form below.

☐	THE ASCENT OF RUM DOODLE	W. E. Bowman	£1.75
☐	THE COMPLETE NAFF GUIDE	Bryson, Fitzherbert and Legris	£2.50
☐	SWEET AND SOUR LABRADOR	Jasper Carrott	£1.50
☐	GULLIBLE'S TRAVELS	Billy Connolly	£1.75
☐	THE MALADY LINGERS ON	Les Dawson	£1.25
☐	A. J. WENTWORTH	H. F. Ellis	£1.60
☐	THE CUSTARD STOPS AT HATFIELD	Kenny Everett	£1.75
☐	BUREAUCRATS — HOW TO ANNOY THEM	R. T. Fishall	£1.25
☐	THE ART OF COARSE RUGBY	Michael Green	£1.75
☐	THE ARMCHAIR ANARCHIST'S ALMANAC	Mike Harding	£1.60
☐	CHRISTMAS ALREADY?	Gray Jolliffe	£1.25
☐	THE JUNKET MAN	Christopher Matthew	£1.75
☐	FLASH FILSTRUP	Peter Plant	£1.00
☐	A LEG IN THE WIND	Ralph Steadman	£1.75
☐	TALES FROM A LONG ROOM	Peter Tinniswood	£1.75

Postage _____

Total _____

ARROW BOOKS, BOOKSERVICE BY POST, PO BOX 29, DOUGLAS, ISLE OF MAN, BRITISH ISLES

Please enclose a cheque or postal order made out to Arrow Books Ltd for the amount due including 15p per book for postage and packing both for orders within the UK and for overseas orders.

Please print clearly

NAME ....

ADDRESS ....

....

Whilst every effort is made to keep prices down and to keep popular books in print, Arrow Books cannot guarantee that prices will be the same as those advertised here or that the books will be available.